• REDISCOVERING RAILWAYS •

SURREY

The west of the county

Southern and London Midland and Scottish Railway Companies
SOMERSET AND DORSET RAILWAY JOINT COMMITTEE.
(8/28) S. & D. Stock 787
TO
SURBITON
S.R.

London Brighton & South Coast Railway.
Hayling Island to
GODALMING
(L. & S.W.R., via HAVANT).

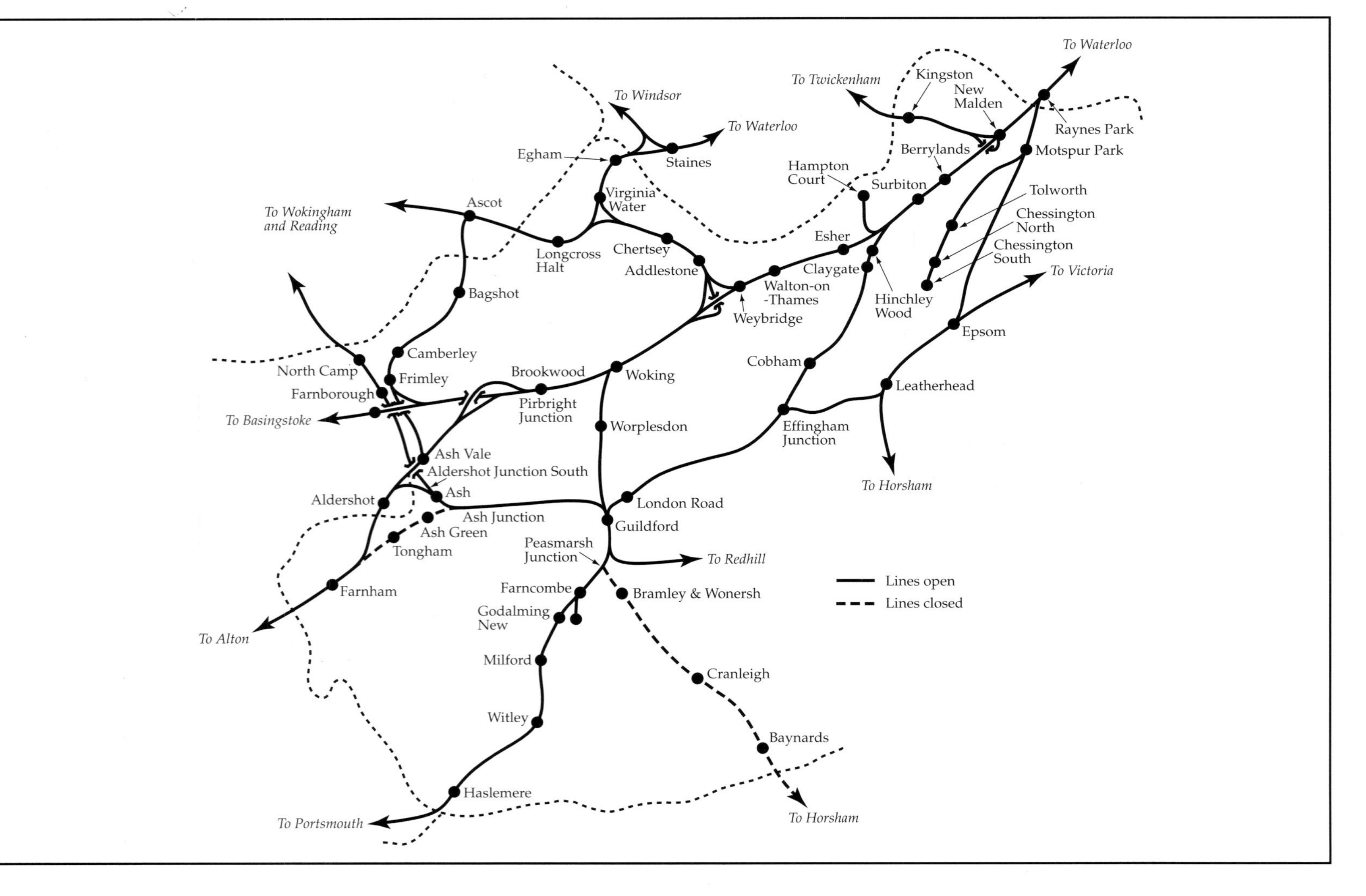

Map of the railways of west Surrey, showing the principal locations and others illustrated in the book. The railways of Epsom, Leatherhead, the Redhill line east of Guildford and other locations eastward are included in the companion volume dealing with the east of the county.

• REDISCOVERING RAILWAYS •

SURREY

The west of the county

A pictorial record of the area's railways past and present

Terry Gough

London and South Western Railway

Date 8.11.19

From WOKING

To Robertsbridge SER

Route Via G'ford

Owner & No. of Wagon 39743

Owner & No. of Sheet

Owner & No. of Under Sheet

Consignee Beattie

[W. & S. Ltd.]

• RAILWAY HERITAGE •

from

The NOSTALGIA *Collection*

First published in 2002

British Library Cataloguing in Publication Data

A catalogue record for this book is available from the British Library.

ISBN 1 85895 213 1

Past & Present Publishing Ltd
The Trundle
Ringstead Road
Great Addington
Kettering
Northants NN14 4BW

Tel/Fax: 01536 330588
email: sales@nostalgiacollection.com
Website: www.nostalgiacollection.com

Some of the material in this book first appeared in *British Railways Past and Present, No 18 Surrey and West Sussex*, by the same author and published by Past & Present Publishing Ltd in 1993.

All tickets and other items of ephemera are from the author's collection, and all photographs are by the author unless otherwise credited.

Printed and bound in Great Britain

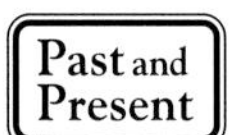

A Past & Present book
from
The* NOSTALGIA *Collection

CONTENTS

WOKING: An up Portsmouth Harbour train is seen at Woking just before the new BR electric multiple units (EMUs) were introduced, with three 4COR units, the leading one being 3149.

Woking was not a traditional stronghold of Class 37 diesels and they were very rarely seen until the mid-1990s. Thereafter they became commonplace, and on 25 April 1995 Nos 37377 and 37194 *British International Freight Association* work an infrastructure train through the up local platform.

ASH JUNCTION: The 4.04pm Redhill to Reading train is worked by Class N No 31819 on 30 May 1963, and is seen passing Ash Junction. The line in the foreground leads to Tongham, by this time freight-only.

In the second view, taken on 23 April 1992, the Tongham line has been taken up. Unit L596 of Class 119 forms the 11.26 Gatwick Airport to Reading service.

INTRODUCTION

I have enjoyed preparing the updated version of this book, which has enabled me to use more of my previously unpublished material. It covers the western part of Surrey, and hence most of the lines are of the former London & South Western Railway (LSWR), later the Western Section of the Southern Region of British Railways. I have taken the county boundary as at the time of the 'past' photographs, and have thus been able to include several suburban lines. The eastern side of Surrey is covered in a companion volume.

Although I was born at Waterloo, Surrey became my home county and Woking my town of residence for over 30 years. This explains in part why I have included so many photographs of the Woking area. A less personal reason is that the area has always been very interesting from a railway point of view, and even today a few hours spent at Woking will often yield interesting workings or motive power. In the 1960s there was almost always activity in the freight and engineers' yards just west of the station. Mail traffic also provided interesting motive power, particularly at Christmas.

Guildford was another location well worth a visit, with its large and latterly run-down station, with adjacent engine shed. It was here that trains from all three Southern Railway (SR) constituent companies met, together with trains from the Western Region, on a regular basis. Guildford shed has of course gone, and the station has been rebuilt.

Motive power and rolling-stock are obviously very different now compared with 40 years ago. Steam vanished in the late 1960s and the main line through Woking was the last in the country to use steam on a daily basis. Since the summer of 1992 there has been a welcome introduction of special steam-hauled passenger trains on the South Western main line and through Guildford. Many of the diesel locomotives that replaced steam are now themselves life-expired and the next generation is taking over. There is no longer any pre-Nationalisation locomotive-hauled rolling-stock in normal passenger service, and even BR Mark I stock has been withdrawn. The last regular locomotive-hauled passenger trains, those to Exeter, were replaced by diesel multiple units (DMUs) in the summer of 1993. All SR-built electric units have been replaced by modern units, the most prestigious being the 'Wessex Electrics'. While the frequency of services has been reduced on some lines, new routes have been introduced.

The contrast between the rural and suburban lines in Surrey is stark. Most of the rural lines have gone, but suburban lines are busier than ever. Indeed, the same applies to the main lines, as people commute further and further distances. This book is a photographic record of these extremes, from the 1960s to the present day.

Terry Gough
Sherborne, Dorset

ACKNOWLEDGEMENTS

I am grateful to the owners of both domestic and commercial private property in granting me access to former railway land. I also thank the railway authorities for giving access to their side of the railway 'fence'. Lawrence Golden is thanked for providing the colour photographs, and I thank my wife Cynthia for her patience when I was away on railway 'business' longer than anticipated.

BIBLIOGRAPHY

The Bisley Branch, Peter A. Harding and John M. Clarke (1986)
The Brookwood Necropolis Railway, John M. Clarke (Oakwood Press, 1983)
The Horsham to Guildford Direct Railway, H. R. Hodd (Oakwood Press, 1975)
London Commuter Lines (2 volumes), Frank Hornby (Silver Link Publishing, 1999)
The Railways of Southern England (3 volumes), Edwin Course (Batsford, 1973/74/76)
The Reading to Tonbridge Line, R. W. Kidner (Oakwood Press, 1978)
Rediscovering Railways: Berkshire, Terry Gough (Past & Present Publishing, 2002)
Rediscovering Railways: Hampshire, The north of the county, Terry Gough (Past & Present Publishing, 2001)
Rediscovering Railways: Surrey, The east of the county, Terry Gough (Past & Present Publishing, 2002)
Southern Railway Reflections: Branch Lines Recalled, Terry Gough (Silver Link Publishing, 1999)
Southern Railway Reflections: Surrey and Berkshire, Terry Gough (Silver Link Publishing, 1999)
A Southern Region Chronology & Record, R. H. Clarke (Oakwood Press, 1964 and 1975)
The Waterloo to Southampton Line, R. W. Kidner (Oakwood Press, 1983)

SOUTH WESTERN SUBURBAN LINES

KINGSTON is host to electric units of Class 4SUB on Christmas Eve 1960. Although both of the same class, they are clearly very different. On the left is No 4311, built by the SR in 1925, and on the right the characteristic shape of the much later Bulleid-designed coaches can be seen. The River Thames, a short distance behind the camera, forms the county boundary.

The present-day service is very frequent with trains running round the loop in both directions from and to Waterloo. In addition, there are trains to and from the Shepperton branch. On 9 September 1999 Class 455 No 5850 works the 16.33 Waterloo to Shepperton service.

MOTSPUR PARK: The station nameboard confirms that this photograph has not been printed the wrong way round, as an ex-LSWR electric unit, SR No 4149, works wrong line through Motspur Park on 1 October 1955 on a Waterloo to Effingham Junction train; the down line was closed for engineering works. The unit was withdrawn two months later.

The present-day train also appears to be on the wrong line, but the indicator is at the rear of the train. This is the 13.18 Epsom to Waterloo service, with Class 455 No 5721.

TOLWORTH (1): This view is from an overbridge built to carry a dual carriageway over the railway between Malden Manor and Tolworth. However, the road was never built and the only traffic now carried is that to a school immediately to the right of the camera. Chessington South and later Tolworth were coal distribution points, and the trains for these were regularly worked by Class Q1 0-6-0s; on 31 October 1962 No 33030 is being used.

These trains ceased to run many years ago, but in 1999 Tolworth goods yard was re-opened for a short period for the distribution of road stone, brought in by rail as required. The more mundane sight of Class 455 No 5851 greeted the author in an unsuccessful attempt to photograph a stone train, which had been cancelled.

TOLWORTH (2): When Tolworth station was closed due to the engineering works mentioned on page 10, the substitute bus service, provided by London Transport's Kingston Depot, was in the hands of No TD106.

Subtle changes have since taken place, as seen in the second view taken in September 1999. The pillar-box has been moved, the top part of the entrance has been sliced off and there is a tree on the roof. The booking office is only open at peak times and tickets are available from the machine at the entrance.

CHESSINGTON NORTH: Steam passenger trains were exceptionally rare on the Chessington branch. This is Class 5MT No 73113 passing through Chessington North with empty carriage stock that will later form the 6.28pm return excursion from Chessington South to Swindon on 25 May 1957. All the stations on the 1939-opened Chessington branch were built to this style.

Class 455 No 5725 leaves Chessington North as the 08.52 all-stations Waterloo to Chessington South service on 10 September 1999. There is a half-hour service throughout the day, with a few extra trains during peak periods.

CHESSINGTON SOUTH (1): Shunting a coal train into the sidings beyond Chessington South station on 22 December 1957 is Class Q1 No 33018. Only the platform on the left has ever been used for passenger trains, and the up platform was never completed. Chessington South is the terminus of the branch, although the line continued for a short distance and earthworks for the planned continuation to Leatherhead were in evidence as far as Chessington Zoo; there was a proposal to lay track on this section and run a tram service from the South station. A London Transport double-deck tram was obtained for this purpose, but remained as a static exhibit in the Zoo grounds until the project was discontinued.

It is peak time in the July 1999 photograph, but with a train recently departed the station looks abandoned.

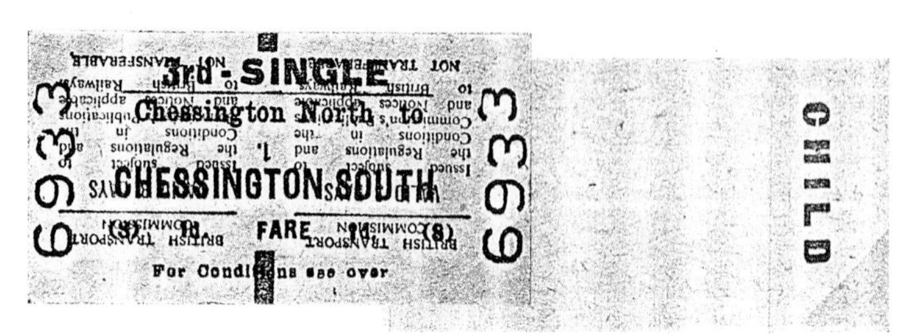

Left Both sides of a misprinted single ticket issued in 1956

CHESSINGTON SOUTH (2): Some excursions in the 1950s were DMU-operated, and on 21 June 1957 one such unit was berthed beyond Chessington South station. It had come from Ipswich earlier in the day, despite displaying Penistone on its indicator blind. The vehicles are E50029 and E56029, built the previous year at Derby, and later referred to as Class 114.

The present-day view gives no indication that the line was ever intended to go through to Leatherhead.

HAMPTON COURT: A contrast in 4SUBs at Hampton Court on 1 October 1955: No 4219 is formed from a three-coach ex-LSWR electric set, later rebuilt as Class 1201, with an ex-LSWR 11-compartment trailer added in 1942. On the right is No 4640 built in 1949. No 4219 was withdrawn at the end of the year and No 4640 was later destroyed in a fire at Effingham Junction.

Trains are now almost exclusively worked by Class 455 EMUs. On 9 September 1999 the 16.09 all-stations service to Waterloo is worked by No 5727.

SOUTH WESTERN MAIN LINE

NEW MALDEN: Bridge replacement at New Malden over the second weekend in May 1960 resulted in wrong-line workings. Here Class 2BIL No 2059 heads a Portsmouth & Southsea to Waterloo train on the down main line, while in the background is the breakdown train headed by Class U No 31796.

The footbridge over the railway is still accessible and on 10 September 1999 Class 4CEP (411) No 1538 is on the up main line forming the 09.10 Portsmouth & Southsea to Waterloo via Eastleigh service. In the station is a Class 455 on a Kingston loop train.

BERRYLANDS is only served by local trains, with no platforms for the centre up and down fast lines. On 8 September 1962 Class 5MT No 73115, showing an Exmouth Junction shed plate, works a Waterloo to Southampton train.

The present-day 12.17 Waterloo to Cardiff Central, operated by Wales & Borders, is only available to passengers travelling to Warminster and beyond, and seat reservation is mandatory. On 9 September 1999 the train is formed of Class 158 No 158820.

SURBITON: A miscellaneous selection of coaches is taken through Surbiton by Class U No 31612 on an empty working from Oatlands Park on 18 August 1962.

The station has remained almost unchanged since building and in 1999 underwent a refurbishment to restore it internally to near original condition. By contrast, the modern office block shown in the 'past' photograph has been demolished and a new (and more attractive) building put up in its place. On 23 November 2001 the 09.16 Alton-Waterloo train, made up of Class 458 No 8012, passes through Surbiton on the up fast line.

ESHER (1): The view from the down local platform on 3 April 1960 shows 'Schools' Class No 30908 *Westminster* with the 10.54am Waterloo to Bournemouth train. On the extreme right is the goods yard.

The original buildings on the down platform survived until 1987, and this 1992 photograph shows some of the extensive alterations to the station that subsequently took place. The platforms have been extended, a footbridge has replaced the subway and, out of view, the entrance to the station has been relocated, while the goods yard has become a car park. The train on the down through line, with EMU Class 421/5 No 1314 leading, is for Portsmouth, and the two trains on the up and down local lines are on the Alton services.

ESHER (2): Looking in the opposite direction, 'Merchant Navy' Class No 35011 *General Steam Navigation* is seen passing through the station on a special train from Portsmouth to the London Midland Region on 10 May 1963. Esher was also frequented by special trains on Sandown Park race days and additional platforms were located beyond the country end of the station on the up side.

On 6 March 1992 Class 423/1 EMU No 3470 passes the same point on an all-stations train from Portsmouth & Southsea to Waterloo.

WALTON-ON-THAMES (1): 'West Country' Class No 34026 *Yes Tor* makes an impressive sight as it rushes through the station on a down West of England express on 18 August 1962. On summer Saturday mornings there was a procession of trains destined for Bournemouth and Weymouth, or Exeter and beyond.

Walton-on-Thames is still recognisable and trains still run to Exeter, in this instance the 15.15 from Waterloo hauled by Class 47/7 No 47716 *Duke of Edinburgh's Award*. However, the signals are now colour lights, the goods shed and yard have gone and the station buildings have been replaced.

Subsequently all passenger trains became multiple-unit-operated, but on 23 March 1995 a 'Wessex Electric' unit was hauled (presumably because of a traction failure) by electro-diesel Class 73 No 73109 *Battle of Britain 50th Anniversary*.

Right WALTON-ON-THAMES (2): Another feature of summer Saturdays was the movement of empty carriage stock from berthing points outside London into Waterloo. Here Class L1 No 31786 hauls empties towards Walton-on-Thames on 5 August 1961.

A much simplified track layout is seen in April 1992, with Class 423 EMU No 3019 on an all-stations train from Southampton.

WALTON-ON-THAMES (3): An up Bournemouth train hauled by 'Battle of Britain' Class No 34071 *601 Squadron* passes Oatlands Park carriage sidings, located at the country end of Walton-on-Thames, on 25 August 1962. The cutting extends to the next station at Weybridge.

In the April 1992 view the sidings have disappeared and trees have invaded right up to the track. Class 423/1 No 3428 forms an all-stations train from Basingstoke to Waterloo.

WEYBRIDGE (1): 'Merchant Navy' Class No 35020 *Bibby Line* on the down 'Bournemouth Belle' passes Weybridge on 5 August 1961. There are still several LSWR relics in evidence, including the bay starter signal, the wooden lamp-post and the yard crane.

In March 1992 there was no sign of the goods yard or semaphore signals. The down platform has been extended and the up bay remains in regular use for the Waterloo via Staines service. A 'Wessex Electric' (Class 442) unit heads for London on the through line.

WEYBRIDGE (2): Electric units of a previous era pass Weybridge on an express to Portsmouth Harbour on 31 July 1963. The leading unit is 4COR No 3116 built by the SR in 1937. The line round to Virginia Water and Staines can be seen on the left of the view.

Present-day Portsmouth trains have less character and are frequently worked by Class 423 units, in this instance led by No 3020. Since the summer of 1992 the best trains are often worked by 'Wessex Electrics'.

WOKING (1): A wet day in October 1964 reveals a dismal sight – steam locomotives en route for scrap. In this instance it is the pre-Grouping engine hauling two BR-built Class 4MT tank engines. The leading engine is Class M7 No 30053, which ironically survived and can now be seen heading trains on the Swanage Railway. In the up bay on the far left are two 2BIL electric units. The bay on the right was exclusively for mail traffic.

Both bays have since been filled in, although there are still sidings in the right middle distance for berthing electric stock. On 24 March 1995 Class 47 No 47767 works an empty stock train through Woking.

WOKING (2): Despite the modern image, this is a 'past' shot. The short-sightedness of selling the land formerly used for the up bay was finally realised in the 1990s; with the through platforms at full capacity and more people than ever commuting to London, it became necessary to re-instate an up bay, which was achieved by re-aligning the down lines and building a new terminal line between the up and down fast lines. The work began in the autumn of 1996, and here Class 37 No 37371 works a china clay slurry train from Quidhampton past the site of the new platform.

The new platform is seen in use on 2 February 2000, with a member of Class 455 forming the 11.15 stopping train to Waterloo.

WOKING (3): The evening vans train from Waterloo to Southampton was frequently worked by a member of Class S15, and on 15 July 1963 it was the turn of No 30840. This train was loaded from the down country-end bay at Woking, which was also used by a few passenger trains per day.

In the bay on 22 May 1994 is the very unusual sight of a motor luggage van. It is Class 419 No 9003, built at Eastleigh in 1960. These vehicles never worked in this area in revenue-earning service, but when this photograph was taken it had been transferred to departmental stock. The bay is still in use, mainly for berthing South West Trains' only locomotive on standby to rescue failed trains.

WOKING (4): Good views of Woking Engineers' Yard were to be had from the country end of the down local platform. From here on 15 October 1960 'Battle of Britain' Class No 34051 *Winston Churchill* is seen setting back a train of ballast wagons into the yard, having just arrived from Meldon Quarry.

Steam is still seen occasionally at Woking. On 24 March 1995 'Merchant Navy' Class No 35028 *Clan Line* takes a commuter train to Waterloo to mark the 100th anniversary of Woking Borough Council.

WOKING (5): An unusual EMU formation was in use between Woking and Basingstoke in the spring of 1995, in the form of No 930082. This three-coach route-learning unit was formerly Class 4CEP No 1505, and is seen approaching Woking on 25 April.

A recent innovation has been a service between Basingstoke and East Anglia via Feltham and Stratford. On 5 December 2001 Anglia Railways Class 170 No 170207 leaves Woking forming the 07.38 Norwich to Basingstoke service. This service is due to be withdrawn in September 2002, due to lack of patronage.

34101
436
397

Passenger lift
Other platforms and way out

Opposite WOKING (6): On 25 July 1964 the Waterloo to Basingstoke stopping train is worked by 'West Country' Class No 34101 *Hartland*, rather a mean train for such an engine. It is waiting to depart from the down local platform.

On 5 October 1996 Class 37 No 37046 brings a ballast train into the same platform. Note that the centre platform number has been changed from 4 to 3: since the opening of the new London-end bay, the platform has reverted to its former number.

WOKING (7): A unique event – SR electric locomotive Class CC No 20002 approaches Woking from Portsmouth with the Royal Train in May 1965.

For a short period in 1988 during the transition from using REP EMUs to the introduction of the 'Wessex Electrics', some of the Bournemouth trains were locomotive-hauled using Class 73s in pairs. This is the 15.53 Weymouth to Waterloo train approaching Woking in June 1988 with Nos 73104 and 73107.

There is a daily train of empty oil tanks from Eastleigh to Holybourne (near Alton), and this reverses at Woking. It runs late in the evening and can therefore only be photographed satisfactorily in midsummer. It is seen here arriving at Woking on 17 July 1996 behind Class 60 No 60083.

WOKING ENGINEERS' YARD: In the yard on 5 July 1964 is Class S15 No 30834 hauling a Class 08 diesel shunter and a more conventional assortment of wagons.

In the same location on 15 April 1993 are a Class 37 on a ballast train in the yard, with Class 60 No 60024 on the oil train from Eastleigh on the up local line. The latter had been temporarily retimed to run in the late morning.

WOKING FREIGHT YARD (1) was situated on the opposite (down) side of the line. On 30 December 1963 Class S15 No 30833 has just arrived on a freight train. The threat of imminent dieselisation is represented by No D6583 (later Class 33/0 No 33063).

Some changes to the skyline of Woking are apparent, and the railway has also changed; the old freight yard is now a second engineers' and aggregates yard and the goods shed is out of use. Another Class 33, this time No 33116 *Hertfordshire Rail Tours*, is seen in the yard on 8 August 1996, but its days are nearly over. Adjacent is Class 59 No 59101, which has just arrived on a stone train from Merehead.

WOKING FREIGHT YARD (2): In the yard on 3 July 1966 is Class 4MT No 76033 on a train of bolster wagons. The Portsmouth line is on the immediate left and the West of England line is further left, between the electricity sub-station and the engineers' yard.

On 9 October 1992 the Merehead stone train is worked by Class 56 No 56116, seen here setting back into the yard prior to unloading.

WOKING JUNCTION (1): Just beyond Woking Junction is a footbridge that spans both the Portsmouth and Weymouth/Exeter lines. On 25 July 1964 'Battle of Britain' Class No 34109 *Sir Trafford Leigh-Mallory* negotiates the junction with the 3.35pm Waterloo to Bournemouth train composed of a rake of Bulleid coaches. The freight yard is on the far right.

On 25 September 1988 electro-diesel Class 73 No 73010 passes the junction on the down local line hauling two Southern Region DMUs.

WOKING JUNCTION (2): A re-enactment of history took place on 26 September 1987 when two SR electric units were seen on the up local line at Woking. The rear (nearest the camera) is preserved Class 2BIL No 2090 showing an inappropriate 'tail' code, namely Waterloo to Strawberry Hill. The leading unit is 4SUB No 4732.

A modern diesel locomotive is seen at the same place on the evening of 16 August 1996, as Class 58 No 58037 heads toward Holybourne with the evening empty oil wagons.

ST JOHNS, WOKING: Beyond Woking the railway enters a deep cutting that opens out at St Johns, where this photograph was taken. An extraordinary event was recorded on 20 July 1963 when BR Standard Class 9F No 92239 worked the 6.22am Bournemouth Central to Waterloo train. However, these engines were not permitted to work into Waterloo because of the tight curves, and on this occasion the train was terminated at Woking. The other train is the 7.20am from Bournemouth West hauled by a 'Battle of Britain' Class, unidentified in the excitement! The two trains were normally scheduled to arrive at Waterloo at 10.20am and 10.00am respectively.

The same location on 14 May 1992 shows Class 47/0 No 47241 on the 05.30 Yeovil Junction to Waterloo train.

BROOKWOOD (1): The 7.02pm Waterloo to Southampton vans train, headed by Class S15 No 30835, passes under the LSWR signal gantry at the London end of Brookwood on 25 July 1963.

There is still an interesting evening working and this is in the form of a Woking to Eastleigh infrastructure train. On 13 June 1996 this is in the hands of Class 37 No 37798.

BROOKWOOD (2): 'Merchant Navy' Class No 35003 *Royal Mail* makes an impressive sight tearing through the station on the 7.30am Exeter Central to Waterloo train on 13 July 1963. The Necropolis branch bay was at the other end of the station to the left of the signal box, and the Bisley branch bay was at the same end, on the up side.

Little has changed at Brookwood apart from the loss of the signal gantry and box and the addition of the third rail to the through lines. Class 47/7 No 47714 makes an unscheduled stop on 20 November 1991 with the 09.28 from Exeter St David's to Waterloo in connection with engineering works, prior to reversing on to the down line to gain access to Woking by 'wrong line working'.

PIRBRIGHT JUNCTION (1): A good view of the railway is available immediately west of Pirbright Junction. The 'past' shot is typical of the 1950s and 1960s, with a Class U 'Mogul', No 31797, on an up slow train. The same location today sees a succession of multiple units, but on 24 March 1995 steam returned briefly in the form of 'Merchant Navy' Class No 35028 *Clan Line*.

PIRBRIGHT JUNCTION (1): The track-level view in the opposite direction is less attractive. On 17 August 1963 Class 4MT No 76065 is seen on the 2.54pm Waterloo to Basingstoke stopping train.

An unusual electric unit fitted with a pantograph appeared in the Woking area in March 1995. This was No 316997 and was coupled to a 4CEP unit to test new central-locking mechanisms for slam-door trains. No 316977 was built at Eastleigh in 1956 and converted to 25kV overhead collection in 1960. It was allocated to the Eastern Region until taken out of public service.

DEEPCUT CUTTING (1): In steam days Bulleid 'Pacifics' were of course commonplace. This is 'West Country' Class No 34040 *Crewkerne* on the 9.22am Bournemouth West to Waterloo train in Deepcut Cutting on 1 June 1963.

The only locomotives now normally seen are diesels on freight trains. On 21 August 1996 Class 37 No 37042 works a china clay slurry train from Quidhampton.

DEEPCUT CUTTING (2): Just prior to entering the cutting and crossing the county boundary, the main line curves gracefully, giving an excellent view of down trains. Here 'West Country' Class No 34039 *Boscastle* and a Bulleid set are seen on the 'Royal Wessex' on 10 August 1963.

Another named train, on this occasion the 'Bournemouth Belle' hauled by Class 33/0 33008 *Eastleigh*, is seen on 25 July 1987. This is, of course, the VSOE version of the 'Belle', the regular service train operated by BR having been withdrawn 20 years earlier.

PORTSMOUTH LINE

NEAR WOKING: A once common sight throughout the British Isles was the cattle train. Movement of livestock had been a long-standing commitment of the railways, but early in the 1960s the decision was made to stop conveying cattle and within a short time cattle wagons had all but disappeared from the railway scene. In this photograph, taken on the Portsmouth line near Woking on 20 December 1962, an unidentified SR 'Mogul' hauls a freight train, consisting predominantly of cattle wagons, towards London.

Interesting trains are still occasionally seen passing this location. On 15 May 1996 a weedkilling train is hauled by Class 20 No 20904 *Janis*. Sister engine No 20901 *Nancy* is on the rear. Note the housing development to the right and the additional facilities for the sidings on the left.

SMARTS HEATH lies between Woking and Worplesdon and there is a good view of the railway looking north. In dreadful weather on 22 December 1962 Class M7 No 30055 takes a parcels train from Woking to Guildford.

The same location with much better weather on 2 April 1997 finds Class 37 No 37133 on an infrastructure train from Woking to Three Bridges.

WORPLESDON is the first station beyond Woking on the Portsmouth line, and it has retained its country atmosphere despite being well within the South East commuter area. The sidings located at the country end of the station were being taken out in October 1964 and the signal box was demolished shortly afterwards. Track relaying through the station is also taking place, and the lifting equipment is being hauled by Class 5MT No 73160.

There is now little trace of the sidings, and the platforms have been lengthened to accommodate 12-coach trains. The station no longer has a Sunday service, and on 8 March 1992 the 14.13 Portsmouth Harbour to Waterloo train, formed of Class 421/5 No 1302, passes through.

GUILDFORD (1): Immediately north of Guildford the Portsmouth line is joined by the New Line from Surbiton to Guildford via Effingham Junction (on the right), and by the ex-SECR line from Reading (left). On 22 August 1964 Class U No 31790 descends into Guildford with a freight train from Reading.

On 25 April 1992 Class 101 No L842 passes the same point forming the 15.10 service to Redhill.

GUILDFORD (2): This is the 15.30 Portsmouth Harbour to Waterloo train on 3 July 1987. The extraordinary formation of a Class 50, No 50018 *Resolution*, and Mark II coaches, instead of the usual EMUs, ran during the summer of 1987, and was the result of Plymouth Laira Depot being responsible for providing rolling-stock and motive power for all Waterloo-Exeter trains. This particular set was used on a Paignton to Portsmouth working in the morning and was required to work a Waterloo to Exeter train later in the day.

The 'past' and 'present' photographs have not been reversed! This shot of *Clan Line* leaving Guildford was taken nine years later, on 22 March 1996. The 'Pacific' is working the VSOE train on a half-day tour from London and back via the North Downs Line.

GUILDFORD (2): An excellent view is obtained from the road overbridge at the south end of Guildford station, as a Horsham train leaves from platform 2 on 18 October 1964. On the extreme left is the corrugated asbestos coaling plant, just visible behind platform 7, while above it in the background is Guildford Cathedral.

A great deal of change is apparent from this viewpoint today. The station has been completely rebuilt with a relocated and far better entrance hall, being officially re-opened on 8 December 1990. An office block (as yet unoccupied) has been built on the extreme right, and on the opposite side the coaling plant area and yard are now car parks, although a few sidings have been retained for berthing purposes. The Cathedral still dominates the skyline, but in contrast to most locations there are far fewer trees in the 'present' view than before. Class 101 No L834 leaves on a Gatwick Airport train, while Class 423/1 No 3430 and Class 455/7 No 5721 wait to leave on up fast and slow trains respectively.

GUILDFORD (3): Looking south from the same bridge gave an excellent view of the engine sheds, which comprised a long shed and a half-roundhouse. Passing the sheds on 15 May 1964 is Class N No 31400 on the 5.04pm Redhill to Reading train. Perched over the tunnel is a crane engaged in building construction.

Thirty-two years later the engine shed site has become a multi-storey car park and the crane has finished its business. The Redhill to Reading services are operated by DMUs, in this instance Class 166 No 166221, forming the 14.26 Gatwick Airport to Reading on 23 February 1996.

PEASMARSH JUNCTION in April 1965 finds Class 2MT No 41294 coming off the Horsham branch. This line closed in 1965, but the Portsmouth line on the right is still very much alive.

The remains of the junction were photographed in January 1992; although hidden from view, the steps from the road bridge still exist, but lead nowhere. Class 421/5 No 1302 passes on a Waterloo to Portsmouth Harbour service.

FARNCOMBE was the first station beyond Guildford on the Portsmouth line, and it is seen here under repair in 1967; 2BIL No 2152 is the rear unit of a Waterloo-bound train. The station has recently been given new nameboards and lamp standards.

In March 1992 Class 421/5 No 1306 works the 11.20 Waterloo to Portsmouth Harbour service. Nameboards and lamp standards have been replaced again and the footbridge has lost its canopy, but little else has changed.

GODALMING station is most attractive and apart from the introduction of double yellow lines and some street furniture including Victorian-style 'gas' lamps (!), there is little to indicate a span of 30 years between these photographs.

MILFORD: Not much has changed here either over 30 years. The bicycle shed is now an open-air affair, the level crossing gates behind the camera are now automatic barriers and the signal box has been demolished. The train is the 11.45 Portsmouth & Southsea to Waterloo service, worked by Class 423 No 3154 on 1 March 1992.

WITLEY station is in a delightful setting. The 'past' view shows a then recently introduced 4VEP (now Class 423), No 7750, on an up train. The station is still gas-lit and has Southern Railway 'totem' nameplates.

Although the station buildings are still the same, today the furniture has been replaced and the platforms refaced. Class 421/2 No 1220 works the 12.20 Waterloo to Portsmouth Harbour service.

HASLEMERE is the last station on the Portsmouth line in Surrey, and it is seen here in 1967 and 1997, with virtually no alterations. Even the signal box (right) is still in use. It is interesting, however, that beyond Haslemere some of the stations have been completely rebuilt.

In the present-day view, Class 4BEP (412) No 2301 forms the 10.20 Waterloo to Portsmouth Harbour service. On the left is Class 20 No 20902 *Lorna* on a weedkilling train, which followed the passenger train as far as Fratton.

SOUTH WESTERN SECONDARY LINES

NEAR ADDLESTONE: There were several freight trains daily between Feltham Yard and the South Western main line via Chertsey. On 31 July 1963 one such train is being worked by Class Q1 No 33010.

The scene had altered significantly by April 1992. There are now only occasional freightliners and Feltham Yard has closed. Passenger trains are mainly in the hands of sliding-door suburban stock, in this instance a Class 455 on a Waterloo to Guildford train. Through trains to Woking and Guildford were withdrawn a few weeks later and all trains ran to Weybridge as was the custom until 1986. A limited service was re-instated in 1993, and, from May 2000, the new Basingstoke to East Anglia service. What was once an attractive view has been ruined not only by natural growth but also by the hut in the foreground and a new feeder road to the M25 motorway.

CHERTSEY YARD had a daily freight, seen here waiting to leave for Weybridge on the morning of 8 May 1963 behind Class S15 No 30507. To the left is the water tower of the engine shed, which was closed in 1937. The 'Underground' sign on the right is a mystery, as the nearest station is Richmond, 18 miles away. Chertsey level crossing and station are in the background.

The view on 24 April 1992 was totally different. The engine shed site and goods yard had both been taken over by small industrial developments. However, the station is still open and the automatic barrier for the level crossing can just be seen.

VIRGINIA WATER (1): A freight train heading for Woking, hauled most unusually by a 'Battle of Britain' Class, No 34087 *145 Squadron*, comes off the Virginia Water east curve in May 1965. The splitting signal in the foreground is for the Reading (via west curve) and Staines lines.

Thirty-one years later Class 47 No 47783 works a Victoria to Southampton Docks boat train past the same point. The signal box has gone and the west curve was taken out in 1966, but there is a proposal to re-instate it to enable through workings between Woking and Reading.

VIRGINIA WATER (2): There is plenty of SR ironmongery in this 1967 view. The east curve to Chertsey is in the foreground and to the right is platform 2 for Reading.

Modernisation has come to Virginia Water, as can be seen on 1 April 1992. Unfortunately none of the indicators are working, the clock is several minutes fast and the next train to Woking was cancelled. Empty stock used its path!

LONGCROSS HALT: A special train to Reading and beyond approaches Longcross Halt on 12 October 1963. The leading engine is Class T9 No 120 in LSWR livery.

Longcross is currently served only by trains at peak hours. In August 1996 Class 4VEP (423) No 3455 will pass through on a Waterloo to Reading train. Most halts on the SR (apart from the South Coast line) did not issue platform tickets, but for some unexplained reason Longcross started issuing platform tickets in 1965, and the ticket illustrated here is the first ever issued, on 20 May.

BAGSHOT (1): Thirty-three years separate these photographs, but time has had almost no effect on Bagshot station, apart from damage to the canopy, modern signalling and a few minor alterations. On 20 June 2001 Class 73 No 73109 *Battle of Britain 50th Anniversary* runs light through Bagshot on its journey from Woking to Ascot.

BAGSHOT (2): Outside the station the story is the same. The gentlemen's toilet has been demolished but British Telecom has yet to replace its red telephone box. There is even a 1960s car parked outside the station in both 1967 and 1992!

CAMBERLEY (1): What a contrast here, the next station on the line, where everything has changed since 1967. The only item to connect the two views is the station footbridge, just visible in the 'past' view beyond the station building and in the 'present' one behind the platform 1 sign. The glass building in the foreground is the new booking hall.

CAMBERLEY (2): These two views on the railway side of the fence are more obviously of the same place, particularly with reference to the trees and goods bay. On 21 October 1961 the bay is in use and Class 700 No 30698 has just arrived to collect a few wagons.

In March 1992 the goods yard is occupied by cars and the only trains are those on the Ascot to Guildford passenger services, on this occasion Class 423/1 No 3427.

FRIMLEY: Steam came here fleetingly on 15 October 1960, when Class M7 No 30028 arrived on a special train from Farnborough.

Now all that is seen is a succession of electric units, such as Class 423 No 3003 working the 15.32 Guildford to Ascot service on 5 April 1992. The only noticeable addition to the station is a new entrance, tastefully matching the original platform canopy.

ASH VALE station is built on an embankment. The 'past' view shows an unattractive pre-Grouping station made worse by a more recent corrugated iron shed. In the background is 2BIL No 2021 on an Ascot train. The line beyond the train diverges, to the left leading to Ascot and straight ahead to Pirbright Junction and Woking.

Since then the station has been totally rebuilt, although the present structure is hardly more attractive. It is already beginning to look scruffy, with contributions from spray-can operators. The train is the 11.34 Alton to Waterloo service, worked by Class 458 No 8015 on 14 November 2001.

FARNHAM: I had travelled to Farnham on 31 May 1962 in the hope of seeing an ex-LSWR Class 700 0-6-0 on the local freight train. This did not run, so I boarded an electric train to return home. Just at that moment a down electric train, 4BIG No 7101, arrived, steam-hauled by No 30325.

My visit on 23 April 1992 was far less exciting; the 14.26 from Waterloo is being worked by Class 423 No 3034 under its own power.

CLAYGATE: The New Line from Surbiton to Guildford via Effingham Junction was built 40 years after the main line via Woking. Claygate was the first station on the New Line until the SR built Hinchley Wood in 1930. Claygate has not changed much as can be seen from these two photographs. In the first, the Tuesdays-only goods from Surbiton to Cobham passes through Claygate in 1964 behind Class U No 31798.

Present-day trains consist of a succession of modern suburban stock, usually of Class 455. Occasionally main-line trains are diverted this way, which is what has happened in October 1995 as a train of 'Wessex Electric' units from Waterloo to Bournemouth speeds through the station. *Lawrence Golden/TG*

COBHAM was another attractive LSWR station with a small goods yard, where Class Q1 No 33018 is shunting in April 1965. The station is to the right of the goods shed.

A visit on 11 January 1992 revealed that much has changed, except for the presence of a Morris Minor in exactly the same position! The pylon is not new, but is hidden behind the 'Q1' in the older photograph. The coal staithes were located where the lamp-posts now stand.

EFFINGHAM JUNCTION: The New Line only saw steam passenger trains on special occasions, such as when the main line was closed for engineering works. This was the case on 14 March 1965 when 'Battle of Britain' Class No 34060 *25 Squadron* worked a Waterloo to Bournemouth train, seen passing Effingham Junction station. In the background is the electric depot.

Another unusual working, this time in the summer of 1992, was when the weedkilling train visited the line. Class 20s Nos 20901 *Nancy* and 20904 *Janis* take the train towards Effingham Junction en route to Epsom on 5 August 1992.

LONDON ROAD, GUILDFORD (1): Midwinter on the New Line, and an extraordinary sight on 25 January 1959 as Class 0395 No 30567 approaches London Road with the 'Portsmouth Centenarian'.

Dramatic changes in the services on the New Line have taken place. As well as the traditional Guildford to Waterloo service, an hourly service was introduced in 1990 between Guildford and Luton via Leatherhead and West Croydon, but the service ceased to run from the summer of 1994. Dual voltage Class 319 No 319058 works an afternoon train from Luton on 25 April 1992.

LONDON ROAD, GUILDFORD (2): The station is at the end of the cutting and is still an attractive location in 1992 with virtually no changes over 25 years; even the platform surface has not been relaid since cables were put down in 1968. EMU No 319058 returns to Luton as the 15.20 from Guildford on 25 April 1992.

GUILDFORD TO HORSHAM LINE

PEASMARSH JUNCTION: The Guildford to Horsham branch left the ex-LSWR Portsmouth main line at Peasmarsh Junction (see also page 53) and curved sharply towards Bramley. On 8 June 1963 Standard Class 2MT No 41261 works the 10.34am from Guildford past the signal guarding the junction.

Following closure much of the trackbed has been made accessible to the public. A canopy of trees has grown up along the line and there is little to show that the present-day view is of the same place, other than the remains of the telegraph pole and the base of the signal, which is just out of sight.

PEASMARSH TO BRAMLEY (1): On 22 August 1964 another Class 2MT, No 41294, is working a train from Horsham and is seen about half a mile from the junction. This location is now on National Trust land, which leads to the River Wey.

PEASMARSH TO BRAMLEY (2): Crossing the River Wey on 8 June 1963 is the 9.57am Cranleigh to Guildford train, hauled by No 41261. Towards the end of steam all trains were worked by LMS-designed tank engines and the line was never taken over by diesels.

The view in the early spring of 1992 shows that the bridge has been removed. The footpath along the trackbed from Peasmarsh Junction follows the river from here as the land on the left bank is privately owned.

BRAMLEY & WONERSH: Prior to the introduction of the ex-LMS engines, most trains were push-pull operated either by Class M7 or H tank engines. Here Class H No 31530 propels its train out of Bramley toward Horsham on 2 April 1960, passing the Saturdays-only Cranleigh to Guildford service.

On 18 January 1992 there is no sign of a train, despite the presence of the station nameboard and a passenger. From here the Downs Link, a long-distance footpath, uses the trackbed to Christ's Hospital, where it picks up the course of the Horsham to Brighton line. The station buildings at Bramley have all gone and the old station entrance is occupied by small businesses.

CRANLEIGH (1): On 24 March 1961 the 12.09pm Horsham to Guildford train is worked by Class 2MT No 41303, seen leaving Cranleigh with a two-coach Maunsell set, converted by BR for push-pull operation.

Total obliteration of the railway at this point made the location of the 'past' view difficult to determine. The trackbed followed approximately the white line in the car park, and the station buildings were just to the right of the tall white buildings in the background, which are now part of an arcade of shops with flats above. Pressure to re-open the line from here to Guildford resulted in a feasibility study in conjunction with the Local Authority. Unfortunately it has been decided not to proceed with the proposal.

2nd-SINGLE SINGLE-2nd
5229 Baynards to 5229
Baynards Cranleigh | Baynards Cranleigh
CRANLEIGH
(S) 8d. FARE 8d. (S)
For conditions see over | For conditions see over

CRANLEIGH (2): On 24 March 1961 Standard Class 2MT No 41303 arrives with the 12.09pm Guildford-Horsham service. This was a leisurely journey, taking an hour to cover the 19½ miles. Cranleigh was the major station on the line, but the poor service coupled with easy road access to Guildford resulted in closure on 14 June 1965.

By 1992 all evidence of the station had long since been obliterated, except for a gate in the former goods yard. The site is now a car park and shopping centre, and the only link between the two photographs is the row of cottages in the left background.

BAYNARDS was in a beautiful setting, and here Class E4 No 32475 pulls away with a Horsham-bound train in March 1961. These engines were not regularly used on the branch, as they were not push-pull fitted.

The station buildings all survive to the present day; they are privately owned and have been attractively restored. Even the goods shed still stands and the level crossing gates are still in existence, although not on public view. Just beyond Baynards is the line's only tunnel, but this is now blocked off; the Downs Link makes a short diversion to the other side.

GUILDFORD TO READING LINE

ASH JUNCTION: The line just glimpsed amongst the grass in the foreground forms one side of a triangle to Aldershot via Tongham on the Farnham line. This line was closed to passengers in 1937, but freight services were retained as far as Tongham until 1961. Class N No 31826 approaches the junction from the Ash direction on a mixed train on 30 May 1963.

The line to Tongham is now a footpath and the railway is viewed from a slightly different angle through a telephoto lens. Class 119 No L575 works the 12.10 Reading to Redhill service in April 1992.

ASH: With the way forward barred, Class N No 31868 waits with the 1.50pm from Reading. There was a small engine shed here, which, although closed in 1946, still stands and is used by a local company. The signal in the background guards a short bay.

The station buildings have since been demolished and the gates replaced by barriers. Class 119 No L595 forms the 13.10 Reading to Guildford train on 23 April 1992.

ALDERSHOT JUNCTION SOUTH: A Reading-bound train hauled by Class N No 31408 crosses the Basingstoke Canal just before Aldershot Junction South on the last day of 1964. The location is still readily accessible along the towpath, and on 18 February 1995 a Class 165 DMU is reflected in the water.

31910

Way out
FW
52

NORTH CAMP (1) is the last station in Surrey and the line crosses county boundaries several times beyond here. In the first photograph Class U1 No 31910 enters the station from Reading on the 1.30pm to Redhill on 30 May 1963.

The line still has a regular service and the second photograph, taken on 23 April 1992, shows minimal changes apart from the usual modernisation of signals and level crossing barriers, while the siding has been retained to give access to an oil depot. Class 119 No L594 works the 14.33 Reading to Gatwick Airport service.

Since then the main road has been diverted and now crosses the railway by bridge. The level crossing is used only by local traffic, including the competing bus, seen on 4 June 1998.

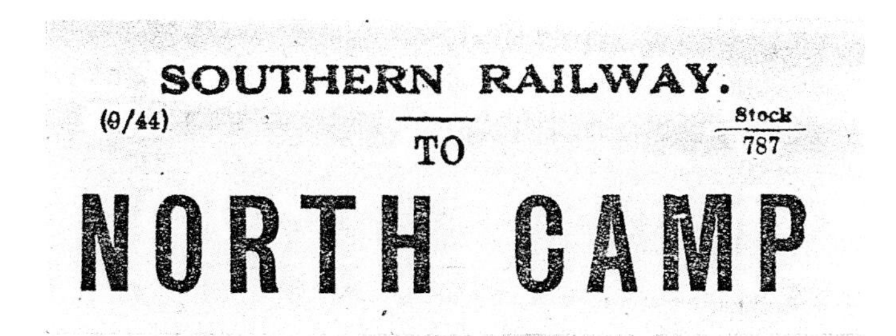

NORTH CAMP (2): An oil train has just arrived on 9 November 1992, and Class 37 No 37888 has deposited the wagons by the oil storage tanks. The crew will return to Guildford on the next service train and a new crew will take over later in the day. On the right is the 09.20 Gatwick Airport to Reading train, formed of unit No L402 of Class 117.

Significant changes have occurred here also, with closure of the oil depot and demolition of the old waiting shelter. A new building is in the course of erection on the depot site on 4 June 1998.

GAZETTEER OF WEST SURREY'S RAILWAYS

Mileages are taken from the Southern Region Passenger Services Timetable, 12 September 1960. Stations were opened and closed on the same dates as their respective lines, unless otherwise stated.

South Western suburban lines

Kingston Loop (LSWR)

Stations in Surrey: Norbiton (11¼m from Waterloo), Kingston (12¼m); Richmond (17¼m), North Sheen (18¼m) and Mortlake (19m).
Opening and closure: Malden (now New Malden) to Kingston (new station) opened 1.1.1869, Kingston to Twickenham 1.7.1863, Twickenham to Richmond 22.8.1848 and Richmond to Mortlake (as part of the line from Clapham Junction) 27.7.1846. An up curve from the Kingston loop to Malden opened 25.3.1883.
Electric trains were due to start running on the Loop 5.12.1915, but were delayed until 30.1.1916. North Sheen opened 6.7.1930.
Route and traffic: This is a very useful but scenically uninspiring line that passes under the main line immediately beyond Malden station. The only interesting features are the crossings of the River Thames at Kingston and Richmond. The line serves a densely populated area and has always had frequent passenger services. Until the 1960s there was also a small amount of freight traffic, particularly for Kingston.

Chessington branch (SR)

Stations: Motspur Park (9¾m from Waterloo), Malden Manor (11m), Tolworth (12m), Chessington North (13¼m), Chessington South (14m).
Opening and closure: Motspur Park opened 12.7.1925. Motspur Park to Tolworth opened 29.5.1938 and Tolworth to Chessington South 28.5.1939. The line was electrified from the outset.
Route and traffic: The junction is within half a mile of Motspur Park station, where the branch turns sharply to the west. There is a more gentle curve on the approach to Malden Manor from where the line continues in a south-westerly direction. The line climbs towards Malden Manor, falls and rises again to Tolworth and repeats this to Chessington North, the steepest being at 1 in 96. It was intended that the line would join the existing railway at Leatherhead, but the intervention of the Second World War resulted in abandonment beyond Chessington South. The stations are of precast concrete to a German design. Traffic was always intended to be predominantly passenger and this is its function to the present day. In addition to local residents, many passengers have come from much further afield to visit what was known as Chessington Zoo. There were goods yards at Tolworth and Chessington South, both of which were exclusively for coal in later years. Tolworth Yard re-opened during 1999 for stone trains.

Hampton Court branch (LSWR)

Stations: Thames Ditton (14m from Waterloo), Hampton Court (15m).
Opening and closure: Opened from Hampton Court Junction, on the main line, to Hampton Court 1.2.1849. Thames Ditton opened in 11.1851. A flyover was installed at Hampton Court Junction 4.7.1915. The branch was electrified 18.6.1916.
Route and traffic: The down line crosses the

main line by means of a flyover. The line is both flat and straight beyond Hampton Court Junction. It was built mainly for passengers and serves the dual function of transporting local people to work and bringing visitors from further afield to Hampton Court Palace. There was a daily goods train until the 1960s.

South Western main line (LSWR)

Stations: New Malden (9¾m from Waterloo), Berrylands (11m), Surbiton (12m), Esher (14½m), Hersham (16m), Walton-on-Thames (17m), Weybridge (19m), West Weybridge (20½m), West Byfleet (21¾m), Woking (24¼m), Brookwood (28m), Pirbright Junction (no station; 29½m), Sturt Lane Junctions (no station, county boundary; 32½m).

Opening and closure: Nine Elms to Woking Common officially opened 19.5.1838, and to the public 21.5.1838. Woking Common to Shapley Heath (now Winchfield) opened 24.9.1838. A down flyunder opened at Byfleet Junction 19.2.1903. An up flyover opened at Pirbright Junction 30.6.1901.

There were very short branches from Brookwood to Bisley Camp (opened 14.7.1890 and closed 21.7.1952), and to Brookwood Cemetery (opened as the Brookwood Necropolis Railway 13.12.1854 and closed 1941). The Bisley branch was extended by the War Department to Pirbright, Deepcut and Blackdown Camps in 1917.

Malden to Hampton Court Junction was electrified 18.6.1916, Hampton Court Junction to Pirbright Junction (and Farnham) 3.1.1937, Pirbright Junction to Sturt Lane Junctions (local lines) 1.1.1939, and Pirbright Junction (all lines) to Basingstoke 2.1.1967. A full electric service between London and Hampshire did not begin until 10.7.1967.

New Malden opened as Malden in 12.1846. It was renamed New Malden & Combe in 5.1859, Combe & Malden until 1.3.1862, then reverted to Malden in 11.1912 and finally became New Malden 16.9.1957. Berrylands opened 16.10.1933, and Hersham 28.9.1936. Surbiton opened as Kingston with the line, and was re-sited in 1845 and renamed Kingston Junction in 12.1852, then Surbiton & Kingston 1.7.1865, and finally Surbiton from 5.1877. Esher was opened as Ditton Marsh with the line, and has had four subsequent name changes, the longest-lived being Esher for Sandown Park, which it retained into the BR period. Walton-on-Thames was called Walton for Hersham until 30.9.1935. West Weybridge (Byfleet & New Haw from 12.6.1961) opened 10.7.1927. West Byfleet opened as Byfleet & Woodham in 12.1887, changed to Byfleet for Woodham & Pyrford in 5.1914 and to its present name 5.10.1950. Woking opened as Woking Common. Brookwood opened 1.6.1864.

Route and traffic: A very well engineered line with no sharp curves or severe gradients, it is ideally suited to fast running. The line runs mostly in a south-westerly direction across the county. Split-level junctions ensure the minimum disruption to through traffic and obviate the necessity for speed restrictions. Traffic is very heavy and even with two up and two down lines, congestion can still occur. Until Byfleet Junction is reached the trains are almost exclusively passenger, but beyond here freight is fairly common. All the goods yards are closed, other than at Woking where there is a stone depot and engineers' yard.

Portsmouth line (LSWR)

Stations: Worplesdon (26¾m from Waterloo), Guildford (30¼m), Shalford Junction (no station; 31½m), Peasmarsh Junction (no station; 32m), Farncombe (33½m), Godalming (34m), Godalming (New) (34½m), Milford (36¼m), Witley (38½m), Haslemere (43m).

Opening and closure: Woking to Guildford opened 5.5.1845, Guildford to Godalming 15.10.1849 and Godalming (New) to Havant 1.1.1859. Worplesdon opened 1.3.1883 and Farncombe 1.5.1897; on the same day the original station at Godalming closed. Witley was called Witley for Chiddingfold until 6.10.1947.

Electrification to Guildford was from 3.1.1937 and to Haslemere (and Portsmouth) from 4.7.1937.
Route and traffic: The line turns sharply south at Woking, and although it is a fairly straight run to Guildford there are some gradients. After passing through tunnels in the Wey Gap, the line reaches Shalford Junction (for Redhill) and Peasmarsh Junction (formerly for Horsham). The original line terminated at Godalming and the station site subsequently became a goods yard. The line climbs out of the Wey Valley from Godalming to the summit at Haslemere. The line is now used exclusively by passenger trains, which have always predominated over freight. The several lines radiating from Guildford ensure a high flow of traffic to and from the Portsmouth line. Apart from this, and commuters from the various intermediate stations, the line carries many people to and from the Isle of Wight.

South Western secondary lines (LSWR)

Weybridge to Staines (LSWR)

Stations: Addlestone (20¾m from Waterloo), Chertsey (22¼ m), Virginia Water (24¾m), Egham (27m); Staines is in Middlesex.
Opening and closure: Weybridge to Chertsey opened 14.2.1848, Chertsey to Virginia Water 1.10.1866. The section to Staines had opened 4.6.1856 as part of the Staines to Ascot line. Access to the Chertsey loop for up trains from the main line was provided by a spur from Byfleet Junction to Addlestone Junction on 4.7.1887. This was closed to passengers 30.1.1916, but now enjoys a regular service again. A flyunder at Byfleet Junction for down trains to the main line was opened 19.2.1903. The line was electrified 3.1.1937. The west curve at Virginia Water, which gave direct access from Chertsey to Reading, closed 26.6.1966.
Route and traffic: The line is built on low-lying land with no significant gradients. There are sharp curves both at Weybridge and Virginia Water where speed restrictions are in force. Apart from the towns themselves, the area through which the line passes has not been developed for housing and is mainly agricultural. Beyond Virginia Water there is more domestic and industrial development. Frequent passenger trains are interspersed with freight several times each day, mostly to and from the Southampton area.

Virginia Water to Farnham (LSWR)

Stations in Surrey: Virginia Water (23¼m from Waterloo direct), Longcross Halt (25¼m); Bagshot (32¼m), Camberley (35½m), Frimley (37¾m), Ash Vale (41m by this route, or 32½m direct); Farnham (38m direct). Sunningdale (27m) and Ascot (29m) are in Berkshire, Aldershot (35m) in Hampshire.
Opening and closure: Staines to Ascot opened 4.6.1856, Ascot to Sturt Lane Junction (on the South Western main line) 18.3.1878, Frimley Junction to Ash Vale 2.6.1879, Ash Vale to Farnham (opened from Pirbright Junction) 2.5.1870.
Electrification took place from Virginia Water to Ash Vale via Ascot 1.1.1939, including connections with the main line at Sturt Lane Junction. Woking to Farnham was electrified 3.1.1937.
Longcross Halt opened 21.9.1942. Camberley was called Camberley & York Town until 9.7.1923, and Ash Vale was North Camp & Ash Vale until 30.3.1924. Farnham was opened 8.10.1849 (see 'Guildford to Reading line' section below). Sturt Lane West spur closed to passengers 4.7.1937. Both Sturt Lane Junctions closed completely in 1967.
Route and traffic: The line passes along the edge of Chobham Common, where Longcross Halt serves a military establishment. Immediately beyond Ascot the line turns sharply south through wooded country to Bagshot. It passes over Bagshot Heath to Camberley and thereafter runs parallel with the Guildford to Reading line in the Blackwater Valley. It passes the site of Frimley and Sturt Lane Junctions just prior to going under the main line. It then follows the Basingstoke Canal to Ash Vale. Much of the heathland to the east of the line is used for military training, and from Ash Vale towards Farnham there are many

army establishments. There are no longer any goods services on the line and revenue is derived from both civilian and military passengers. There are very large increases in passengers on race days at Ascot, and during Ascot Week, special trains are runs from various parts of the country.

Surbiton to Guildford via New Line (LSWR)

Stations: Hinchley Wood (14m from Waterloo), Claygate (15¼m), Oxshott (17m), Cobham & Stoke d'Abernon (18¾m), Effingham Junction (21m), Horsley (22m), Clandon (25¼m), London Road (28½m), Guildford (29m).

Opening and closure: The line opened throughout 2.2.1885. Effingham Junction opened 2.7.1888. An up flyunder opened at Hampton Court Junction 21.10.1908.

The line was electrified from Hampton Court Junction to Claygate 20.11.1916 and on to Guildford 12.7.1925. Hinchley Wood opened 20.10.1930. Oxshott was opened as Oxshott & Fairmile.

Route and traffic: The line serves the affluent towns in the traditional Surrey 'stockbroker belt'. Between the towns the line passes through relatively unspoilt and pleasant countryside. A frequent electric train service has been provided for over 75 years.

Guildford (Peasmarsh Junction) to Horsham (LBSCR)

Stations in Surrey: Peasmarsh Junction (no station; 1¾m from Guildford), Bramley & Wonersh (3¼m), Cranleigh (8¼m), Baynards (11¼m); remaining stations were in Sussex.

Opening and closure: The line was opened throughout 2.10.1865 and closed completely 14.6.1965. Bramley & Wonersh was plain Bramley until 1.6.1888. Cranleigh was Cranley until 6.1867.

Route and traffic: From Peasmarsh Junction the line headed south-east, close to a tributary of the River Wey almost to Cranleigh. Beyond there it climbed to the highest point on the line just beyond the isolated station of Baynards and the county boundary. The line was lightly used by both passengers and freight, the main commodities being bricks and fuller's earth. Most passenger trains traversed the whole length of the branch to Horsham, although there were a few trains which ran only between Guildford and Cranleigh

Guildford to Reading line (LSWR/SECR), including Tongham line (LSWR)

Stations: Wanborough (4¼m from Guildford), Ash Junction (no station; 5¾m), Ash Green (6m), Tongham (7¼m); Ash (6¼m from Guildford), Aldershot Junction South (no station; 7m), North Camp (8¼m); remaining stations are in Berkshire and Hampshire.

Opening and closure: Guildford to Ash Junction (LSWR) and Ash Junction to North Camp and Farnborough North (SECR) both opened 20.8.1849. Ash Junction to Farnham via Tongham (LSWR) opened 8.10.1849; it closed to passengers 4.7.1937 and completely 2.1.1961. Ash to Aldershot spur (LSWR, Aldershot Junction South to Aldershot Junction North) opened 1.5.1879. Frimley Junction to Ash Vale (LSWR) opened 2.6.1879. Guildford to Aldershot via the Aldershot Junctions was electrified 1.1.1939. The line from Aldershot Junction South to North Camp and beyond is not electrified (until Wokingham is reached).

Wanborough opened 1.9.1891, Tongham in 10.1856. Ash was named Ash & Aldershot to 9.1858, Aldershot (Ash) to 6.1859, Ash & Aldershot to 6.1863, and Ash Junction to 11.1926. North Camp opened as North Camp Aldershot in 1858. It retained this name until 6.1863 when it became Aldershot Camp. It changed to Aldershot (North Camp) in 5.1879, then to Aldershot (North Camp) & South Farnborough in 6.1910, to Aldershot (North) 9.7.1923, before gaining its present name 30.3.1924.

Route and traffic: There is a long climb on a curve out of Guildford to reach Broadstreet Common and Wanborough. The line continues over mostly common and farmland until Ash, which is the beginning of a built-up area that extends through to North Camp. Just before Aldershot Junction South it crosses the Basingstoke Canal and enters the Blackwater Valley. Traffic has traditionally been a mixture of freight and passenger. Freight was both local and long-distance through Reading. There is much local civilian and military passenger traffic, augmented by through trains to the Kent Coast and in more recent years a frequent service to Gatwick Airport.

AUGUST 31st

11.40 a.m. EXCURSION

Maidenhead, Taplow, Burnham (Bucks), Windsor and Eton Central, Slough, Langley (Bucks), Iver, West Drayton and Yiewsley, Hayes & Harlington and Southall

TO

CHESSINGTON SOUTH

Return Train leaves Chessington South at 6.26 p.m.

INDEX OF LOCATIONS

Page numbers in **bold** refer to the photographs; other entries refer to the Gazetteer section.